D1015583

Cat Rules

Virtues of the Feline Character

© 2002 Willow Creek Press

Cover and title page photo: © Terry Wild Studio

Published by Willow Creek Press
P.O. Box 147
Minocqua, Wisconsin 54548

Edited by Andrea Donner

Printed in Canada

Cat Rules

Virtues of the Feline Character

Willow Creek® PRESS

$\mathcal{C}$ats are angels with fur.

SARK

enchanting

*C*ats simply ought not to go about radiating such distracting charm.

BEVERLY NICHOLS

5

𝒰nlike us, cats never outgrow their delight in cat capacities, nor do they settle finally for limitations. Cats, I think, live out their lives fulfilling their expectations.

IRVING TOWNSEND

*I*f man could be crossed with the cat, it would improve man but deteriorate the cat.

MARK TWAIN

$\mathcal{A}$n ordinary kitten will ask more questions than any five year old.

CARL VAN VECHTEN

8

I am indebted to the cat for a particular kind of honorable deceit, for a greater control over myself, for a characteristic aversion to brutal sounds, and for the need to keep silent for long periods of time.

COLETTE

serene

Cats know everything there is to know about meditation.

VERONIQUE VIENNE

© Robert Kaufman/Silver Visions

10

*K*ittens are born with their eyes shut. They open them in about six days, take a look around, then close them again for the better part of their natural lives.

STEPHEN BAKER

*I*f a dog jumps in your lap, it is because he is fond of you; but if a cat does the same thing, it is because your lap is warmer.

ALFRED NORTH WHITEHEAD

$\mathcal{C}$ats are connoisseurs of comfort.

JAMES HERRIOT

Cats are intended to teach us that not everything in nature has a function.

GARRISON KEILOR

© Bonnie Nance

$\mathcal{C}$ ats are rather delicate creatures and they are subject to a good many different ailments, but I have never heard of one who suffered from insomnia.

JOSEPH WOOD KRUTCH

There is nothing sweeter than his peace when at rest, for there is nothing brisker than his life when in motion.

CHRISTOPHER SMART

*E*verything that moves serves to interest and amuse a cat.

F.A. Paradis De Moncrof

$\mathcal{H}$e alone is
an acute observer
who can observe
minutely without
being observed.

JOHN CASPER
LAVATER

© Walter Chandoha

$\mathcal{T}$he curious
are always in
some danger. If
you are curious
you might never
come home.

JEANETTE
WINTERSON

© LouisaPreston.com

𝒜 kitten is chiefly remarkable for rushing about like mad at nothing whatever, and generally stopping before it gets there.

AGNES REPPLIER

℧ost of us rather like our cats to have a streak of wickedness. I should not feel quite easy in the company of any cat that walked about the house with a saintly expression . . .

BEVERLY NICHOLS

21

elegant

$\mathcal{L}$ike a
graceful
vase, a cat,
even when
motionless,
seems to flow.
GEORGE WILL

23

$\mathcal{T}$o err is human, to purr is feline.

ROBERT BYRNE

There is no need for a piece of sculpture in a home that has a cat.

WESLEY BATES

25

clean

*B*etter keep youself clean and bright; you are the window through which you must see the world.

GEORGE BERNARD SHAW

© Walter Chandoha

27

$\mathcal{T}$he cat has too much spirit to have no heart.

ERNEST MENAUL

*C*at people are different, to the extent that they generally are not conformists. How could they be, with a cat running their lives?

LOUIS J. CAMUTI, DVM

*I*n a cat's eyes,
all things
belong to cats.
ENGLISH
PROVERB

© Terry Wild Studio

30

Cats know how to obtain food without labor, shelter without confinement, and love without penalties.

W.L. GEORGE

31

There are no ordinary cats.

COLETTE

Cats sleep
Anywhere
Any table
Any chair
Top of piano
Window-ledge
In the middle
On the edge.

ELEANOR FARJEON

A cat is the only domestic animal I know who toilet trains itself and does a damned good job of it.

JOSEPH EPSTEIN

© LouisaPreston.com

$\mathcal{A}$ cat's got her own opinion of human beings. She don't say much, but you can tell enough to make you anxious not to hear the whole of it.

JEROME K. JEROME

calm

Only in a quiet mind is adequate perception of the world.

HANS MARGOLIUS

$\mathcal{A}$re cats lazy? Well, more power to them if they are. Which one of us has not entertained the dream of doing just as he likes, when and how he likes, and as much as he likes?

FERNAND MER

How we behave toward cats here below determines our status in heaven.

ROBERT A.
HEINLEIN

39

$\mathcal{N}$o matter how much cats fight, there always seem to be plenty of kittens.

ABRAHAM LINCOLN

*I*f cats
could talk,
they wouldn't.
NAN PORTER

41

C ats are the ultimate narcissists. You can tell this because of all the time they spend on personal grooming. Dogs aren't like this. A dog's idea of personal grooming is to roll in a dead fish.

JAMES GORMAN

© Bonnie Nance

© Bonnie Nance

43

Cleanliness may be recommended as a mark of politeness, as it produces
affection, and as it bears analogy to purity of mind.

JOSEPH ADDISON

Sleep is a reward for some, a punishment for others. For all it is a sanctuary.

COMTE DE LAUTRÉAMONT

Some people say that cats are sneaky, evil, and cruel. True, and they have many other fine qualities as well.

MISSY DIZICK

© Norvia Behling

© Bonnie Nance

$\mathcal{C}$ats do not go for a walk to get somewhere but to explore.

SIDNEY DENHAM

affectionate

Our perfect
companions
never have fewer
than four feet.

COLETTE

© Bonnie Nance

© Terry Wild Studio

*P*urring would seem to be, in her case, an automatic safety-valve device for dealing with happiness overflow.

MONICA EDWARDS

49

$\mathcal{B}$y associating with the cat one only risks becoming richer.

COLETTE

There are two means of refuge from the misery of life—music and cats.

ALBERT SCHWEITZER

*A*ll animals are
equal, but some
animals are more
equal than others.
GEORGE ORWELL

© Walter Chandoha

$\mathcal{L}$ove to eat them mousies
Mousie's what I love to eat.
Bite they little heads off
Nibble on they tiny feet.

B. KLIBAN

53

Cats are absolute individuals, with their own ideas about everything, including the people they own.
JOHN DINGMAN

Cats seem a bridge to a world beyond the one we know.

LYNN HOLLYN

𝒯he smallest feline is
a masterpiece.
LEONARDO DA VINCI

© Randy Handwerger

*I*ndividuality is everywhere to be spared and respected as the root of everything good.

JEAN PAUL RICHTER

Curiosity is the thirst of the soul.

SAMUEL JOHNSON

$\mathcal{W}$hat greater
gift than the love of
my cat?
CHARLES DICKENS

60

© Walter Chandoha

© Walter Chandoha

$\mathcal{W}$e humans are indeed fortunate if we happen to be chosen to be owned by a cat.
ANYONYMOUS

I love cats because I love my home and after a
while they become its visible soul.

JEAN COCTEAU

$\mathcal{I}$t is impossible for a lover of cats to banish these alert, gentle, and discriminating friends, who give us just enough of their regard and complaisance to make us hunger for more.

AGNES REPPLIER

© Walter Chandoha

$\mathcal{T}$he little furry buggers are just deep, deep wells you throw all your emotions into.

BRUCE SCHIMMEL

*I*t is difficult to obtain the friendship of a cat. It is a philosophical animal . . . one that does not place its affections thoughtlessly.

THEOPHILE GAUTIER

67

$\mathcal{T}$housands of years ago, cats were worshipped as gods. Cats have never forgotten this.

ANONYMOUS

© Randy Handwerger

The ideal of calm exists in a sitting cat.

JULES REYNARD

God made the
cat in order that
man might have
the pleasure of
caressing the lion.
FERNAND MERY

© Walter Chandoha

© John Perryman

71

Cats are smarter than dogs. You cannot get eight cats to pull a sled through snow.

JEFF VALDEZ

© Randy Handwerger

© Norvia Behling

C ats seem to go on the principle that it never does any harm to ask for what you want.

JOSEPH WOOD KRUTCH

$\mathcal{T}$hose who will play with cats must expect to be scratched.

MIGUEL DE CERVANTES SAAVEDRA

$\mathcal{M}$ost cats, when they are Out
want to be In,
and vice versa,
and often simultaneously.

DR. LOUIS J. CAMUTI

© John Perryman

A cat is a puzzle
for which there is no
solution.

HAZEL NICHOLSON

$\mathcal{W}$ho can
believe that there
is no soul behind
those luminous
eyes!

THEOPHILE
GAUTIER

© John Perryman

The phrase 'domestic cat' is an oxymoron.

GEORGE WILL

© Randy Handwerger

*P*rowling his own quiet backyard or asleep by the fire, he is still only a whisker away from the wild.

JEAN BURDEN

*Af*ter dark all cats are leopards.

NATIVE AMERICAN
PROVERB (ZUNI)

When a mouse laughs at the cat, there is a hole nearby.

NIGERIAN PROVERB

*W*ho, being
loved, is poor?
OSCAR WILDE

© Walter Chandoha

© John Perryman

$\mathcal{T}$he life of inner peace, being harmonious and without stress, is the easiest type of existence.

NORMAN VINCENT PEALE

$\mathcal{T}$he cat is nature's beauty.

FRENCH PROVERB

© Bonnie Nance

*B*efore a Cat will condescend
To treat you as a trusted friend,
Some little token of esteem
Is needed, like a dish of cream.

T.S. ELIOT

wise

I have studied many philosophers and many cats. The wisdom of cats is infinitely superior.

HIPPOLYTE TAINE

© Sally Weigand

$\mathcal{M}$y cat does
not talk as respect-
fully to me as I do
to her.

COLETTE

$\mathcal{A}$ man has to work so hard so that something of his personality stays alive. A tomcat has it so easy, he has only to spray and his presence is there for years on rainy days.

ALBERT EINSTEIN

*W*hen I play with my cat, who knows if I am not a pastime
to her more than she is to me?

MICHEL DE MONTAIGNE

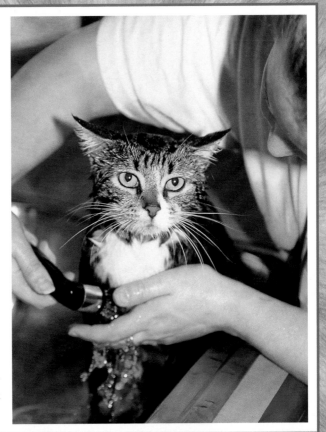

$\mathcal{T}$o bathe a cat takes brute force, perseverance, courage of conviction — and a cat. The last ingredient is usually hardest to come by.

STEPHEN BAKER

© Sally Weigand

93

*C*at: a pygmy lion who loves mice, hates dogs, and patronizes human beings

OLIVER
HERFORD

© Ron Kimball / www.ronkimballstock.com

𝒯he cat does not offer services. The cat offers itself. Of course he wants care and shelter. You don't buy love for nothing. Like all pure creatures, cats are practical.

WILLIAM SEWARD BURROUGHS

$\mathcal{A}$s every cat owner knows, nobody owns a cat.

ELLEN PERRY BERKELEY